scjc

# STICKMEN'S GUIDE TO ENGINEERING

Thanks to the creative team:
Senior Editor: Alice Peebles
Fact Checking: Tim Harris
Design: Perfect Bound Ltd

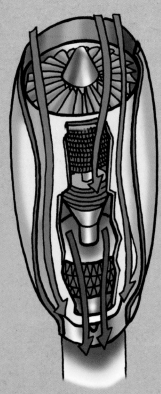

Hungry Tomato®
A division of Lerner Publishing Group, Inc.
241 First Avenue North
Minneapolis, MN 55401 USA

For reading levels and more information, look up
this title at www.lernerbooks.com.

Main body text set in Avenir LT Std 9/5/12.
Typeface provided by Linotype AG.

Library of Congress Cataloging-in-Publication Data

Names: Farndon, John, author. | Matthews, Joe, 1963– illustrator.
Title: Stickmen's guide to engineering / John Farndon ; Joe Matthews
[illustrator].
Description: Minneapolis : Hungry Tomato, [2018] | Series: Stickmen's
guides to STEM | Audience: Ages 8-12. | Audience: Grades 4 to 6.
Identifiers: LCCN 2018006920 (print) | LCCN 2018010804 (ebook) |
ISBN 9781541523951 (eb pdf) | ISBN 9781541500617 (lb : alk. paper)
Subjects: LCSH: Structural engineering—Juvenile literature. |
Engineering—Juvenile fiction.
Classification: LCC TA634 (ebook) | LCC TA634 .F37 2018 (print) |
DDC 620—dc23

LC record available at https://lccn.loc.gov/2018006920

Manufactured in the United States of America
1-43702-33494-4/19/2018

# STICKMEN'S GUIDE

## TO

# ENGINEERING

by John Farndon

Illustrated by Joe Matthews

HUNGRY
TOMATO
Minneapolis

Engineers make everything
that works—including all the
gadgets in your house.

# Contents

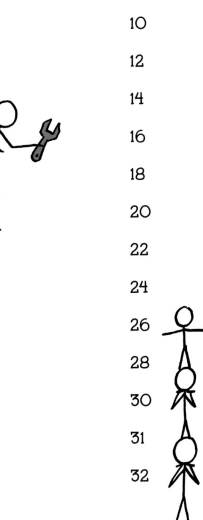

# Introduction

Engineers design structures, machines, and materials. They are the people who come up with the instructions that tell people how to build and make or shape things, from a giant road tunnel to the pipes in your house.

## What do engineers do?

Engineers use science, math, and technical experience to come up with the design for making things. They need to understand the situation properly, then devise a foolproof solution. For example, a heating engineer will design a system that ensures heat reaches all parts of a building.

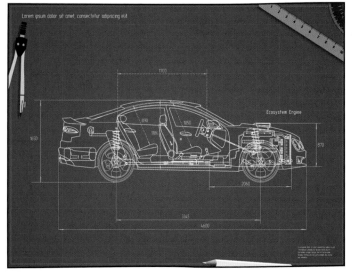

## Blueprints

Engineers usually draw their design in great detail, either on paper or on a computer screen. In the past, they drew their plans on paper and copies were made using a process that made the plans blue. These were called blueprints. Even today, when the copies are black-and-white photocopies, engineering plans are often called blueprints.

## Computer power

Nowadays, engineers prepare their plans using computer-aided design systems (CAD). These are special programs that allow engineers to draw their designs in 3D on screen and make changes quickly if needed. Some CAD programs automatically make calculations about stresses and loads. They can also add up the costs of materials as you go along.

## Megaprojects

Some engineering projects are gigantic, taking many years and involving huge numbers of workers and quantities of materials. These megaprojects include the Jubail II industrial city in Saudi Arabia— a vast city of industrial plants in one place. There are 20,000 workers busy trying to get the project finished by 2026.

## Three Gorges

Sometimes, giant engineering projects can be controversial. The Three Gorges project in China, which was completed in 2003, created the world's largest dam: 1.5 miles (2.4 km) long and about 60 stories high. But its construction involved moving 1.5 million people from their homes and flooding vast areas of farmland.

# Holding It Together

Engineers come up with ideas for useful machines, tools, and structures—and then make them. Science, math, and technology are involved, but engineering is really all about making things that work.

## Going for growth

Airplane

If you live in a city, you're living in an engineer's world. Everything, from the bridge you cross on the way to school to the rack you hang your coat on when you get there, is the work of an engineer. If you look around you as you travel through a city, you'll see examples of engineering everywhere.

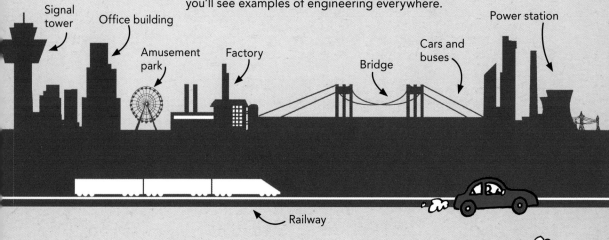

Signal tower

Office building

Amusement park

Factory

Bridge

Cars and buses

Power station

Railway

## Chemical cooks

Chemical engineers focus on processes and equipment for making the chemicals we need, from liquid soap to drugs. They work on all scales, but their most obvious work involves creating large factories for making chemicals and oil refineries for processing oil to make fuel and plastics.

## Keep it civil

Civil engineers are called "civil" to show they are different from military engineers, who make things for war. Civil engineers make big structures that keep cities going, such as roads, airports, bridges, canals, dams, and buildings. Sometimes, they make very big things, such as tunnels under the sea or docks for repairing giant oil tankers.

## Metallic mechanics

Mechanical engineers are engineers who make machines—anything from cars and buses to door handles and graters. They make things that move in some way, and their favorite material is metal because it's tough and can be shaped however they wish.

## Sparks

Electrical engineers design and make electrical equipment—that's everything from mobile phones to power stations and electric trains. They work with wires, electronic circuit chips, and transistors. They need to take care electricity is kept safely out of harm's way with insulating material or by setting wires high up or underground.

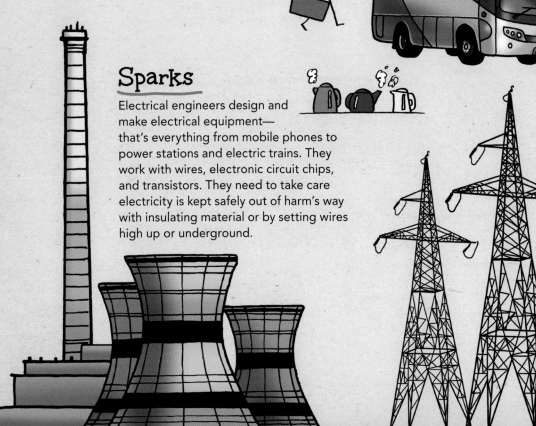

# Make Up

For things to work well, they need to be made from the right material. It's no good building a submarine from wood or a hammer from plastic. An engineer has to find the right material for the task or, if the right material doesn't exist, create a new one.

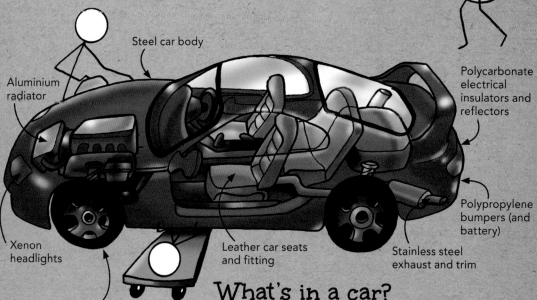

Steel car body

Aluminium radiator

Xenon headlights

Rubber tires (and windscreen wipers and hoses)

Leather car seats and fitting

Polycarbonate electrical insulators and reflectors

Polypropylene bumpers (and battery)

Stainless steel exhaust and trim

## What's in a car?

Cars need to be very strong to stand the stresses of engine power. They also need to be a shape that allows space for passengers and components. That's why they're made mostly of steel, which is both strong and easily shaped when hot. But cars include many other materials, such as glass, rubber, and plastic.

## Making metals

Metals are used for everything from nails to bridge beams and washing machines to ships. If you heat metal enough, it melts. So you can make it into almost any shape by pouring it into a hollow container called a mold. When it cools, the metal turns hard and solid in the shape of the mold. This is called casting.

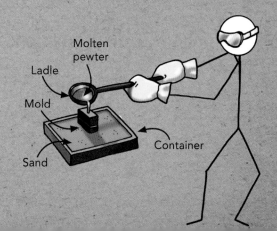

Molten pewter

Ladle

Mold

Sand

Container

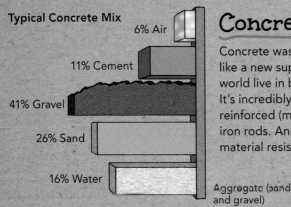

**Typical Concrete Mix**

- 6% Air
- 11% Cement
- 41% Gravel
- 26% Sand
- 16% Water

# Concrete

Concrete was invented long ago, but it's so useful it seems like a new supermaterial. Seven out of ten people in the world live in buildings made at least partly from concrete. It's incredibly strong, especially when reinforced (made stronger) with iron rods. And it's the only building material resistant to fire and water.

Concrete is made by mixing loose sand and gravel, then binding it together with wet powdered cement.

When the cement dries, it sets hard to make solid concrete.

Aggregate (sand and gravel)

Conveyor belt

Concrete supply

Cement store

Concrete mixer truck

Things made from oil

# Out of oil

Oil is not only a fuel; it is a source of an amazing array of materials called petrochemicals. These include everything from the fabric in bedsheets to the plastic in footballs—and even perfumes and drugs. Here are just some of the everyday objects made from oil.

**Materials in a plane, the Boeing 787**

- Carbon laminate
- Carbon sandwich
- Fiberglass
- Aluminium
- Aluminium/steel/titanium pylons

# Combined strengths

**Composites** are amazingly strong, light materials that are made by combining different materials. Typically, they have fibers of glass or carbon embedded in a mass or "matrix" of plastic, metal, ceramic, or even concrete. The fibers strengthen and stiffen the matrix and help it resist cracks and fractures.
Half the Boeing 787 airliner is made of composites.

# We Got the Power!

When you turn on the lights or the TV, you expect electricity to be there to make them work at the flick of a switch. But where does the electricity come from? The answer: it is generated in power stations, then supplied to you through underground wires or sometimes overhead cables.

## Electricity at home

We use a lot of electricity! The average home around the world uses 3,500 kilowatt hours each year—that's enough to boil 3,500 pots of water for an hour. But US households use about four or five times the world average! From the moment we get up, we start using electricity for heat, cooking, light, and many other things.

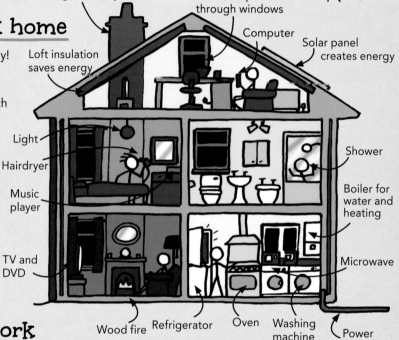

Heat escapes through chimney

Heat escapes through windows

Computer

Solar panel creates energy

Loft insulation saves energy

Light

Hairdryer

Music player

TV and DVD

Shower

Boiler for water and heating

Microwave

Wood fire  Refrigerator  Oven  Washing machine

Power supply

## Power network

Power stations use various sources of energy to turn turbines that power **electricity generators**. They send out their electricity through a network of electric cables called a grid.

**1** Power station generators are connected to the cables of the grid.

**2** To send the electricity long distances, it is boosted to high voltage (pressure) by transformers.

**3** To make the current usable in homes and factories, the voltage is reduced again by more transformers at a substation.

# Burn up

Nearly two-thirds of our electricity is made by power stations that burn fossil fuels. Fossil fuels are coal, oil, and natural gas made from the buried remains of living things. As they burn, they heat water to make steam to turn the generator turbines. But the smoke from burning fossil fuels pollutes the air and changes the world's climate.

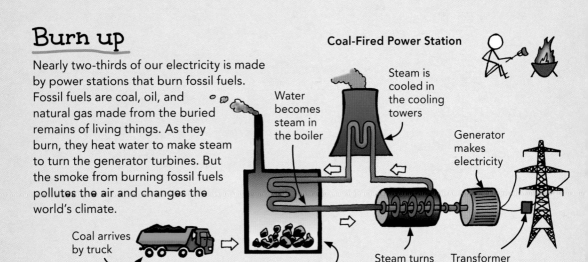

**Coal-Fired Power Station**

Water becomes steam in the boiler

Steam is cooled in the cooling towers

Generator makes electricity

Coal arrives by truck

Coal is burned in the furnace

Steam turns the turbines

Transformer changes voltage

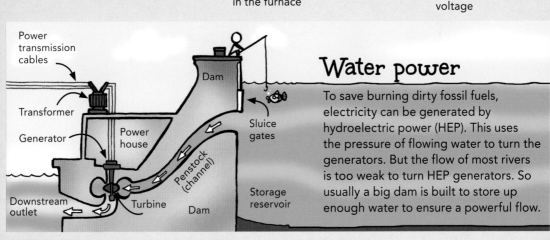

Power transmission cables

Dam

Transformer

Generator

Power house

Sluice gates

Penstock (channel)

Downstream outlet

Turbine

Dam

Storage reservoir

# Water power

To save burning dirty fossil fuels, electricity can be generated by hydroelectric power (HEP). This uses the pressure of flowing water to turn the generators. But the flow of most rivers is too weak to turn HEP generators. So usually a big dam is built to store up enough water to ensure a powerful flow.

# Sunrise

We can also generate electricity from clean alternatives such as wind power and solar power. Solar power uses sunlight to generate electricity in arrays of photovoltaic (PV) cells. PV cells react to sunlight by producing a small current of electricity. The Solar Impulse 2 plane is entirely powered by PV cells.

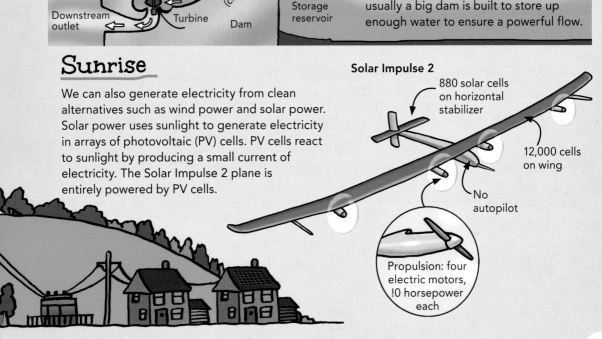

**Solar Impulse 2**

880 solar cells on horizontal stabilizer

12,000 cells on wing

No autopilot

Propulsion: four electric motors, !0 horsepower each

13

# Building Up

In the last century, engineers built more and more awesomely tall buildings called skyscrapers. They were originally built to save space in crowded cities. Now many megatall buildings are erected just to show off!

Solar panels collect energy for the building.

Concrete is strengthened with a mat of thin steel fibers.

## Tall techniques

Most low level buildings get their strength from brick walls. But megatall buildings have very thin walls made mainly of glass, called curtain walls. They get their strength from a superstrong steel frame or spine, to which concrete floors and the curtain wall are attached. They also incorporate clever new techniques.

**Carbon nanotubes** are embedded in the concrete for extra strength.

"Smart" carbon fibers in the concrete send data about stresses.

Elevators can swap shafts to stop holdups.

**Electromagnet** shafts provide quick escape routes in emergencies.

Superfast lifts hauled by carbon-fiber ropes whisk people up at 60 feet (20 m) per second.

## Megatall!

Right now, the world's tallest building is the Burj Khalifa in Dubai, which is 2,717 feet (828 m) and has 163 stories. But when the Kingdom Tower in Saudi Arabia is finished in 2020, it will be over 0.6 miles (1 km) tall! Here's a comparison of the world's tallest buildings. Six of them are in China.

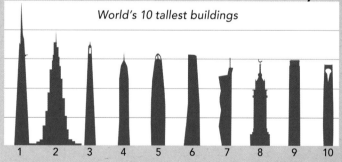

*World's 10 tallest buildings*

1   2   3   4   5   6   7   8   9   10

1 Kingdom Tower, Saudi Arabia
2 Burj Khalifa, UAE
3 Suzhou Zhongnan Center, China
4 Ping An Finance Center, China
5 Wuhan Greenland Center, China
6 Shanghai Tower, China
7 KL118 Tower, Malaysia
8 Makkah Royal Clock Tower Hotel, Saudi Arabia
9 Goldin Finance 117, China
10 Baoneng Shenyang Global Finance Center, China

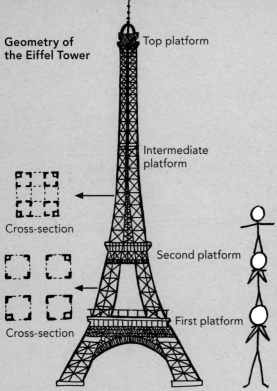

**Geometry of the Eiffel Tower**

Top platform

Intermediate platform

Cross-section

Second platform

Cross-section

First platform

## Metal shapes

When the Eiffel Tower was built in Paris in 1889, it was the world's tallest manmade structure, at 1,063 feet (324 m) tall. Column structures rely on their weight to hold them up. But the Eiffel Tower works by **cantilevers**, which use anchor points. It is made of a geometric lattice of iron girders, each anchored in place by its attachment to others.

## Up and around

Not all tall structures are skyscrapers. The Gateway of St Louis in the US is just an arch for show. But it is the world's tallest, at 630 feet (192 m). It was built out of stainless steel triangular boxes lined with concrete. It has a very special mathematical shape, called a catenary, which gives it strength.

The Gateway Arch, St. Louis

## Elevator to space

You don't necessarily need a building to have an elevator. Some people think that one day we may be able to build an elevator right up into space. A superlight carbon-fiber cable would run from the ground to a weight placed 62,000 miles (100,000 km) above Earth. The weight would hold the cable in place as it orbited Earth. Elevator cars would climb the cable by electromagnets and reach space in just a few hours.

# Getting Across

Bridges are some of the biggest engineering projects of all—
and they are getting bigger all the time. The recently built
Danyang-Kunshan Grand Bridge in China carries a
high-speed railway and is 102.4 miles (164.8 km) long!

## Bridge types

Bridges used to be built
of brick, stone, and iron.
Now most are built from
concrete and steel. To
cross wide rivers or deep
gorges, builders usually
use **suspension bridges**,
which allow for very long,
high spans.

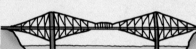
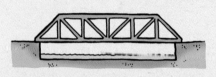

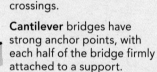
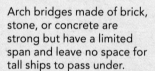

Beam bridges made from
rigid beams of steel are
simple and effective, but only
work well for short crossings
unless they have support in
the middle.

**Truss bridges** are made from
triangles of steel bars. They
are very strong and light,
and a good design for short
crossings.

**Cantilever** bridges have
strong anchor points, with
each half of the bridge firmly
attached to a support.

Arch bridges made of brick,
stone, or concrete are
strong but have a limited
span and leave no space for
tall ships to pass under.

Suspension bridges have a
main span that hangs from
cables suspended between
tall towers at either end.

Cable-stayed bridges have
the main span hanging
directly from cables
attached to towers.

Towers are
constructed
on top of steel
caissons

Steel caisson

## Getting suspended

The key step in building a suspension bridge
is setting up the towers at each end. These
are very tall and take the whole weight of the
bridge. So the foundations must be deep and
built on solid rock. If the towers have to be in
water, engineers start by lowering a vast steel
drum called a caisson into the water. The water
is pumped out of it and keeps everyone safe
and dry while they lay the foundations.

## High bridge

The spectacular Duge Bridge in southwest China is the world's highest bridge. It soars 1,854 feet (565 m) above the Beipan River. It is a cantilever truss bridge, in which the bridge span projects out from two fixed points on either side to join in the middle. Wires called trusses provide extra support.

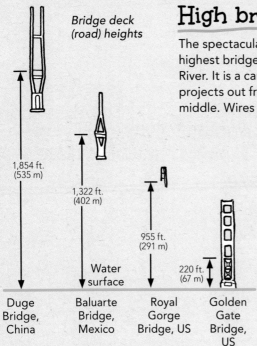

*Bridge deck (road) heights*

1,854 ft. (535 m) — Duge Bridge, China

1,322 ft. (402 m) — Baluarte Bridge, Mexico

Water surface

955 ft. (291 m) — Royal Gorge Bridge, US

220 ft. (67 m) — Golden Gate Bridge, US

Duge Bridge

## Italian bridge

Perhaps the most famous and beautiful bridge in the world is the Rialto in Venice. It was designed by Antonio de Ponte and built between 1588 and 1591. To support the weight of this stone bridge, the builders had to push over 12,000 wooden stumps into the mud. Rows of shops selling fine fabrics, jewelry, and glass occupy the colonnade that sits on the bridge.

## Scotland's Forth

When it was built in 1881, Scotland's railway bridge over the Forth estuary near Edinburgh was the engineering marvel of the age. Built entirely of steel girders, it was the world's longest cantilever bridge. Triangles of steel are anchored to two piers and carry the weight on the bridge.

# Fly Me

One of the newest of all engineering skills is aeronautical engineering, the engineering of aircraft. The Wright brothers made the first successful aircraft flight in 1903. But just over a century later, planes are whisking passengers around the world in hours, and there are flying cars that could land in your garden.

## Air rider

To build a modern airliner, you need three main parts: a **fuselage**, wings, and engines. The fuselage is the long tube where the pilot, passengers, and luggage are carried. Two big wings on either side lift the aircraft, and two little wings and a rudder at the rear provide control. The engines power the aircraft through the air.

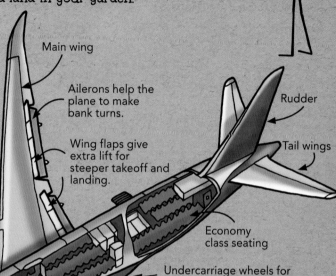

Main wing

Ailerons help the plane to make bank turns.

Wing flaps give extra lift for steeper takeoff and landing.

Rudder

Tail wings

Economy class seating

Undercarriage wheels for landing and takeoff

Business class seating

Jet engines on each wing give power.

**Cockpit** or flight deck

Kitchen galley

## Supertube

The fuselage of an airliner is essentially a tube of superlight, superstrong materials: mainly aluminium, but also titanium and special composite materials like carbon fiber. There is a framework of long beams or "stringers" running along the plane and a series of hoops or "chords" running around it. Metal panels are fixed to the framework to form a "skin."

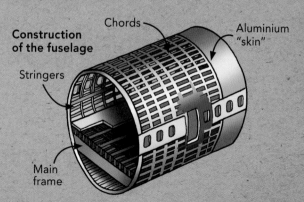

Chords

Aluminium "skin"

**Construction of the fuselage**

Stringers

Main frame

# Wired for flight

When a pilot moves the controls to change direction, a computer sends electrical signals through the wires to motors (actuators) that swivel flaps on the wings. This is called "fly-by-wire." In autopilot, the pilot can leave the controls altogether and the computer makes adjustments to the flight automatically in response to data from the instruments.

**How fly-by-wire controls work**

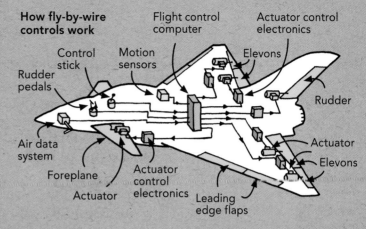

Flight control computer

Actuator control electronics

Control stick

Motion sensors

Elevons

Rudder pedals

Rudder

Air data system

Actuator

Foreplane

Elevons

Actuator

Actuator control electronics

Leading edge flaps

# Flight deck

Airline pilots face a dazzling array of instruments in a plane. The display is sometimes called a "glass cockpit" as it is so full of glass screens showing data readouts, computer updates, and the flight path. The key display is for the FMS (flight management system) computer that automates much of the flight using satellite and other data to guide the aircraft along its flight path.

# Jet power

Most modern airliners are powered through the air by jet engines called **turbofans**. All jets have fans that whir around inside a tube, gulping in air. Turbofans have a second giant fan at the front to suck air in. Because some air bypasses the main fans, the engine runs more quietly at takeoff speeds.

**1** Some of the air is blown into the engine's main fans, but some bypasses them.

**2** Jet fuel is squirted into air squeezed by the main compressor fan (indicated) and set alight.

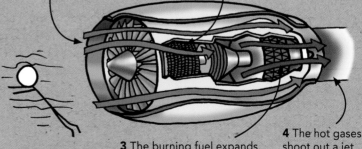

**3** The burning fuel expands and rushes past a turbine, setting it spinning.

**4** The hot gases shoot out a jet that thrusts the plane forward.

# Keeping Afloat

Some ships are the biggest machines of all, and they have to face some of the toughest conditions in the world when they sail into an ocean storm. So a lot of engineering know-how goes into designing and building them. Engineers who work with ships are called marine engineers.

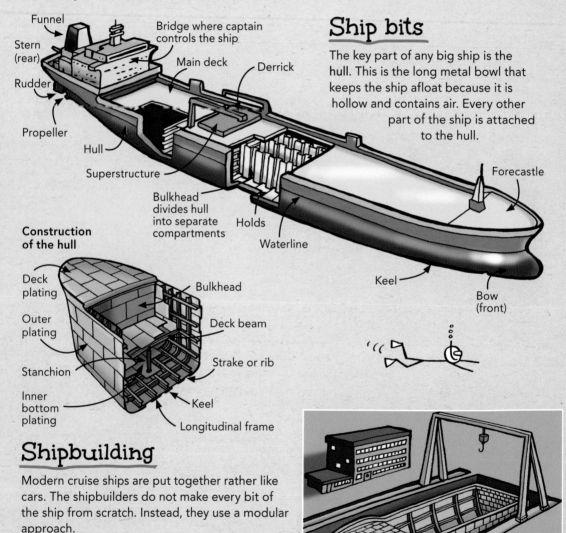

Funnel

Stern (rear)

Rudder

Propeller

Hull

Superstructure

Bridge where captain controls the ship

Main deck

Derrick

Bulkhead divides hull into separate compartments

Holds

Waterline

## Ship bits

The key part of any big ship is the hull. This is the long metal bowl that keeps the ship afloat because it is hollow and contains air. Every other part of the ship is attached to the hull.

Forecastle

Keel

Bow (front)

**Construction of the hull**

Deck plating

Outer plating

Stanchion

Inner bottom plating

Bulkhead

Deck beam

Strake or rib

Keel

Longitudinal frame

## Shipbuilding

Modern cruise ships are put together rather like cars. The shipbuilders do not make every bit of the ship from scratch. Instead, they use a modular approach.

This means they bring in ready-made components, such as passenger cabins and giant sections of steel hull. The components are slowly assembled in a shed until the ship is ready to launch into the water for the finishing stages.

# Boxing clever

Bulk cargo is things such as oil and minerals that can simply be poured into the ship's hold. But loose cargo—objects of all shapes and sizes—poses a problem. The solution is to put it inside standard metal boxes called containers. This way it can be stacked high in specialized ships that are easy to load and unload. This idea works so well that most non-bulk cargo is now carried in container ships.

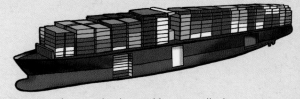

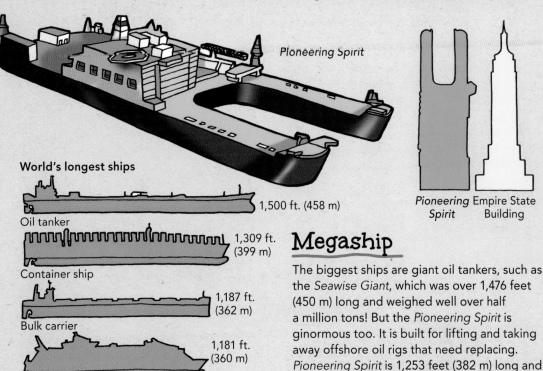

*Pioneering Spirit*

### World's longest ships

1,500 ft. (458 m)
Oil tanker

1,309 ft. (399 m)
Container ship

1,187 ft. (362 m)
Bulk carrier

1,181 ft. (360 m)
Passenger ship

1,118 ft. (341 m)
Aircraft carrier

Pioneering Spirit — Empire State Building

## Megaship

The biggest ships are giant oil tankers, such as the *Seawise Giant*, which was over 1,476 feet (450 m) long and weighed well over half a million tons! But the *Pioneering Spirit* is ginormous too. It is built for lifting and taking away offshore oil rigs that need replacing. *Pioneering Spirit* is 1,253 feet (382 m) long and 406 feet (124 m) wide. See how it compares with the Empire State Building in New York!

## Superyacht

In the future, boats may look rather different. With the latest light, strong materials such as carbon composites, which can be molded in different shapes, boats can be made in interesting new designs. It's just an idea right now, but the *Trilobis*, for instance, has a transparent underwater section, and a silent, non-polluting hydrogen engine, so passengers can observe sea life close up.

# Keep Moving

There are well over one billion cars on the world's roads right now, with 263 million in the United States alone. That's one car for almost every American. So automotive engineers, who design and make cars, buses, and trucks, have a lot of work!

## Car parts

Modern cars are very complicated machines. But most have the same elements: four wheels, a body to carry passengers, an engine to power the wheels, and controls for the driver. The car's power typically comes from burning gas or diesel inside the engine. This expands and pushes firmly on a piston, which turns the shafts that drive the wheels.

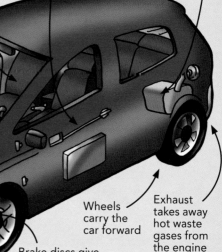

Drive shaft takes the engine's power to the rear wheels

Fuel tank holds the fuel for the engine

Driver's seat

Steering wheel

Engine provides power to move the car

Battery holds store of electricity for when engine is not running

Suspension absorbs bumps in the road

Brake discs give a surface for the brakes to grip and stop the car

Wheels carry the car forward

Exhaust takes away hot waste gases from the engine

## Keeping safe

Nearly 1.3 million people are killed in car accidents every year. So car engineers include features to protect passengers in case of a crash.

Steering column collapses quickly in a crash so as not to crush the driver

Crumple zone at the front, designed to crumple easily and absorb some of the impact

Safety glass breaks into beads rather than sharp splinters

Air bags inflate rapidly to provide a cushion for passengers

Passenger cell, a cage of strong bars, protects the passenger compartment

Safety belts stop passengers hurtling forward violently

## Half clean

When gas and diesel engines burn fuel, they expel a lot of dirty gases that not only damage people's health but also the world's climate. So many carmakers are looking for cleaner ways to power cars. One well-tried idea is the hybrid. This has both a gas engine and an electric motor, sharing the task of powering the car.

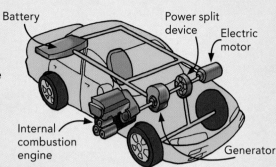

Battery

Power split device

Electric motor

Internal combustion engine

Generator

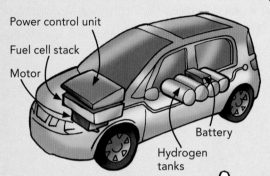

Power control unit

Fuel cell stack

Motor

Battery

Hydrogen tanks

## Water works

Another idea for cleaner engines is the **hydrogen fuel cell**. In some ways, these are like batteries powered by hydrogen. Hydrogen is very flammable, but here it is not burned. Instead, it is combined with oxygen in a process that makes electricity to power an electric motor. Combining oxygen and hydrogen makes water, so the only waste from hydrogen cells is pure water.

## Giant dumper

The biggest dump truck of all is the BelAZ 75710 made in Belarus. It can move almost 550 tons (500 t) of rubble in a single load—about the weight of 250 cars or 40 African elephants! To shift all that, it has an engine with a torque (turning force) 13,738 lb/ft (18,626 Nm)—about 24 times what a 2014 Formula One racing car can do!

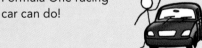

## Shock speed

"Shockwave" is the fastest truck ever. From the front it looks like an ordinary 1984 Peterbilt truck. But three Pratt & Whitney jet engines at the back blast this monster from a standstill to 300 mph (480 km/h) in just 11 seconds. And it can scorch along at 376 mph (605 km/h)!

# On Line

Since the first railway was built just under 200 years ago, engineers have laid 1.4 million miles (2.25 million km) of iron and steel track around the world. Railways are being built all the time—under cities and through mountains, across rivers and deserts . . .

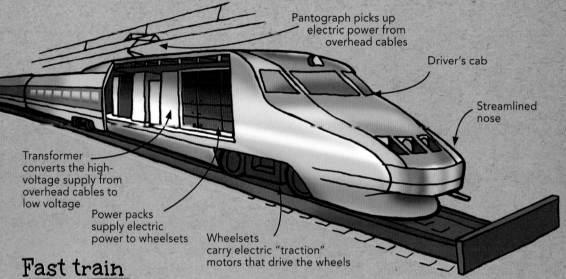

Pantograph picks up electric power from overhead cables

Driver's cab

Streamlined nose

Transformer converts the high-voltage supply from overhead cables to low voltage

Power packs supply electric power to wheelsets

Wheelsets carry electric "traction" motors that drive the wheels

Motor circuits control the flow of electricity and speed of the motors

## Fast train

High speed trains are the fastest way of getting around without actually flying. The fastest trains can reach speeds of 350 mph (560 km/h), much faster than a Formula One racing car. They are powered by electric motors and run on special tracks with only very gentle curves.

Cutting edge at the front with whirring blades that slice through solid rock

Conveyor belt takes waste rock out of the tunnel

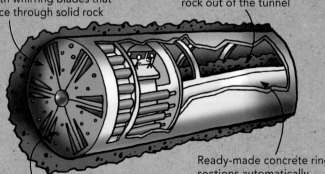

Cutting edge moves slowly forward as rock is bored

Ready-made concrete ring sections automatically pushed into place as the head moves forward

## Going under

In 2016 the Gotthard rail tunnel, the world's longest, was completed under the Alps mountain range in Switzerland. It is over 35 miles (57 km) long! Tunnels like this are bored out with huge machines called Tunnel Boring Machines (TBM), which are like giant drills.

# Magnetic rise

The fastest trains have no wheels and no engine. They are called **maglevs** (short for "magnetic levitation") and use the power of magnetism to float above the track. In 2015, an experimental Japanese maglev reached 375 mph (603 km/h)!

Magnets propel the train forward as well as lift it.

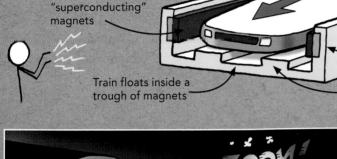
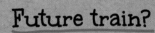

Powerful "superconducting" magnets

Train floats inside a trough of magnets

Magnets in both train and track

# Future train?

The **hyperloop** is an idea for a superfast train. The aim is to shoot passenger-carrying pods at incredible speeds through a tube emptied of air using the power of electromagnets. Test trains have already reached speeds up to 240 mph (387 km/h). They may one day reach speeds of 700 mph (1,134 km/h).

# Making tracks

Trains need tracks to run on. In most designs, flat-bottom steel rails are laid across wooden or concrete support planks called sleepers. The sleepers rest on a bed of crushed stone or "ballast," and the ballast rests on a bed of finer gravel called subgrade.

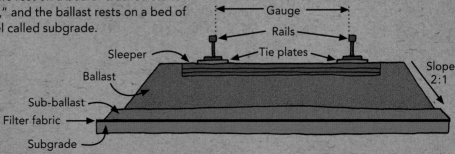

Gauge

Rails

Sleeper

Tie plates

Ballast

Slope 2:1

Sub-ballast

Filter fabric

Subgrade

# Blow Up

Military engineers have always been important for armies. They are sometimes called sappers and it is their task to build things for attack or defense in war. It is also their task to destroy the defenses of the enemy, including walls and minefields.

Warhead with explosives

## Missile launch

Missiles carry explosives toward an enemy target. They have their own motors or rockets to send them on their way and a guidance system to help them hit the target. Some missiles are launched from strongly defended fixed bases. Others are fired from mobile launchers. Some missiles are designed to shoot down enemy missiles.

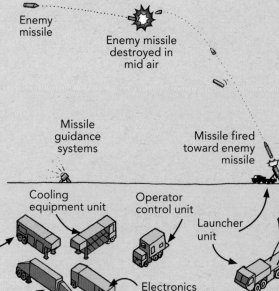

Enemy missile

Enemy missile destroyed in mid air

Missile guidance systems

Missile fired toward enemy missile

Cooling equipment unit

Operator control unit

Launcher unit

Prime power unit

AN/TPY-2 antenna

Electronics equipment unit

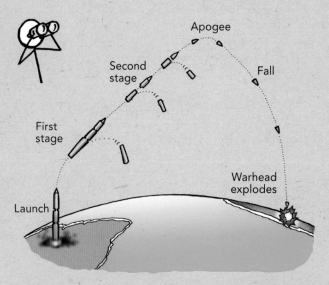

Apogee

Second stage

Fall

First stage

Launch

Warhead explodes

## Continental target

Intercontinental Ballistic Missiles (ICBMs) are missiles that can be fired right across the ocean. To travel that far, ICBMs are fired 500–1,000 miles (800–1,600 km) above the earth by a series of rocket stages. These rocket stages drop away one by one, until the missile reaches its highest point, or "apogee." From there, it simply carries on its path, falling back to earth to deliver its devastating load.

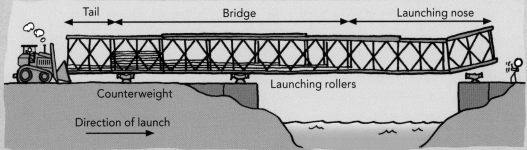

Tail — Bridge — Launching nose

Counterweight

Launching rollers

Direction of launch

# Bridge makers

Sometimes armies find themselves with a river to cross—and no bridge. Maybe the enemy has blown up the only one. Then the army calls in the engineers to set up a temporary bridge called a Bailey bridge. This is made of ready-made sections of truss (steel frames) that can be brought to the site on trucks and then fixed together quickly.

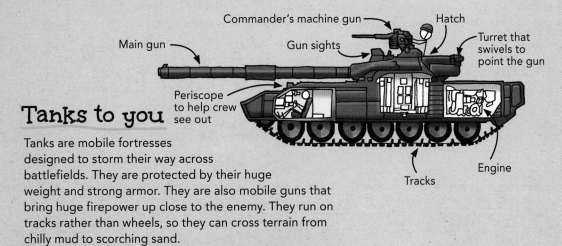

Main gun

Commander's machine gun

Gun sights

Hatch

Turret that swivels to point the gun

Periscope to help crew see out

# Tanks to you

Tanks are mobile fortresses designed to storm their way across battlefields. They are protected by their huge weight and strong armor. They are also mobile guns that bring huge firepower up close to the enemy. They run on tracks rather than wheels, so they can cross terrain from chilly mud to scorching sand.

Tracks

Engine

Balaklava submarine base

# Going to ground

The town of Balaklava on the Black Sea was the site of one of the most amazing feats of military engineering ever. A network of waterfilled passages allowed submarines to sail far in under the mountain. This made a submarine base so strong that it could withstand a direct hit from an atomic bomb!

# Timeline of Engineering

There have been engineers for as long as there have been cities. Ancient civilizations brought together thousands of workers to build giant structures such as aqueducts, pyramids, walls, and bridges. Nowadays, with the aid of machines, steel, and concrete, engineers can build even bigger.

## c.2620 BCE

The first known engineer was the Ancient Egyptian Imhotep, the genius thought to have designed the first pyramid, the Pyramid of Djoser. A giant step for Imhotep.

## 100 CE

The Romans built many amazing aqueducts to carry water from wet hilly areas into cities, including the famous aqueduct bridge at Alcantara in Portugal which still stands. Go flow.

---

**100**      **1700**

---

## c.250 BCE

The greatest engineer of ancient times was Archimedes, who invented the pulley and many other machines, including a claw that could pick up entire ships and shake them about. Want a lift?

## 610

The Grand Canal in China is the world's longest canal, at 1,104 miles (1,776 km). It was begun in the 5th century BCE to link the Yellow and Yangtse rivers, and completed 1,000 years later. Water long time!

## 1206

Islamic engineer Al-Jazari came up with amazing ideas for water clocks and automata, as well as clever systems for moving water about. Bath time.

## 1826

Scottish engineer Thomas Telford built the first great suspension bridge, the Menai Bridge in North Wales, which was for a long time the world's longest bridge. Hang it!

## 1311

Medieval cathedrals were soaring buildings of stone. The tallest of all was Lincoln Cathedral in England, with a spire towering 525 feet (160 m). It blew down in a storm in 1549. That's a point.

## 1889

The Eiffel Tower in Paris was built entirely out of triangles of iron and was the first building ever to reach over 1,000 feet (300 m) in height. Eiffel up.

1800　　　　1900　　　　2000

## 1931

In the early 1900s, New York began to build giant skyscrapers, and the tallest of all was the Empire State Building of 1931, for 40 years the tallest building in the world. Going up!

## 1779

The Iron Bridge in Shropshire, England, was the first major bridge built entirely of cast iron and it signified the start of the Industrial Revolution. Iron cross.

## 2010

Right now the tallest building in the world is the Burj Khalifa tower in Dubai, which has 163 floors and is 2,717 feet (828 m) tall! Gone high.

# Clever!

## Great Wall

The Great Wall of China across the north of the country is the longest wall and largest military defense work in the world. It stretches for 5,500 miles (8,850 km) and has many additional branches. The first wall was built 2,700 years ago, and the most famous one was built 2,200 years ago under Emperor Qin Shi Huang. Most of what you see today, though, was rebuilt during the Ming Dynasty (1368–1644).

## Archimedes's lifter

Greek thinker Archimedes realized the power of levers and pulleys. "Give me a place to stand and I will move the Earth," he told the King of Sicily, knowing that with a lever long enough you can move anything. He proved his point by launching a giant ship on his own using an ingenious arrangement of levers and pulleys—after huge teams of men pulling on ropes together had failed.

## Brunel's smell

Isembard Kingdom Brunel was one of the great engineers of the 1800s and designed steamships, tunnels, and railways. He was very short and he may have worn his tall hat to make himself look taller. Not all of his ideas were brilliant. He once built an experimental vacuum-powered railway, but its mechanism relied on leather that had to be kept supple with smelly tallow. The smell attracted rats which gnawed through the leather.

## Brooklyn heroes

The creation of the mighty Brooklyn Bridge in New York City took a heavy toll on its designers, John and Washington Roebling. Soon after work began, John had a terrible accident on site and died of an infection. A few months later, Washington was also involved in an accident. He was left paralyzed and barely able to speak. But his young wife, Emily, took over the project and saw it through with his advice.

# Glossary

**cantilever:** a long projecting beam or girder fixed at only one end, used in bridge building

**carbon nanotubes:** very tough, microscopic fibers made of carbon and used to make strong, light materials

**cockpit:** the place where a pilot sits and controls a plane. It is also known as the flight deck on large airliners.

**composite:** a material made by combining different materials

**electricity generator:** a machine for making electricity by spinning magnets past coils of electric wire

**electromagnet:** a strong magnet created by sending an electric current through a coil

**fuselage:** the main, tube-shaped body of an airplane

**hull:** the main watertight bowl of a ship that ensures it floats

**hydrogen fuel cell:** a power unit that uses hydrogen to make electricity and power an electric motor. It produces only pure water as waste.

**hyperloop:** a superfast train that uses electromagnets to shoot pods at high speeds through a tube emptied of air

**maglev:** a train that has no wheels but floats above the track by magnetism

**suspension bridge:** a bridge that hangs from cables suspended between tall towers at either end

**truss bridge:** a bridge made from triangles of steel bars

**turbofan:** a jet engine with a second giant fan at the front to suck in air. It creates less engine noise.

# Index

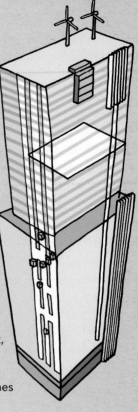

## The Author

John Farndon is Royal Literary Fellow at City & Guilds in
London, UK, and the author of a huge number of books
for adults and children on science, technology, and history,
including such international best-sellers as *Do Not Open* and
*Do You Think You're Clever?* He has been shortlisted six times
for the Royal Society's Young People's Book Prize for titles
such as *How the Earth Works* and *What Happens When?*

## The Illustrator

Self-taught comic artist Joe Matthews drew Ivy The Terrible,
Ball Boy, and Billy Whizz stories for the *Beano* before moving
on to *Tom and Jerry* and *Baby Looney Tunes* comics. He also
worked as a storyboard artist on the BBC TV series *Bob the
Builder*. Joe has produced his own *Funny Monsters Comic*
and in 2016 published his comic-strip version of the Charles
Dickens favorite, *A Christmas Carol*. Joe lives in North Wales,
UK, with his wife.

## Picture credits

**t = top, m = middle, b = bottom,
l = left, r = right**
**Shutterstock:** Anna Phillips
29tr; Atosan 19ml; cocozero
29br; Denys Po 6bl; Gimas 7ml;
Gorodenkoff 7tr; Ilona Ignatova
29br; jejim 7br; Kostenko Maxim 6tr;
omerfarukboyaci 28br; Paul Drabot
23bl; rook76 28bl; Ross Strachan
17bl; rtem 28tr; Steve Bramall 28m;
STLJB 15mr; tourpics_net 29ml;
VPales 27bl; WDG Photo 29mr;
Xavier Fargas 28tl
**highestbridges.com:** 17tr
**Wikimedia Commons:** 29tl
Every effort has been made to
trace the copyright holders. And
we acknowledge in advance for any
unintentional omissions. We would
be pleased to insert the appropriate
acknowledgment in any subsequent
edition of this publication.